Developing Community Partnership Handbook

To Diane!

thank you for
your support and
your encouragement
throughout the years.

Be blessed my Sister,

Dr. Helen Stotts

"Helen"

Developing Community Partnership Handbook

The Repairer of the Breach

Dr. Helen Stafford Fleming

To order additional copies of this book, contact:
Xlibris
1-888-795-4274
www.Xlibris.com
Orders@Xlibris.com
698879

CONTENTS

I dedicate this book to:
Douglas Memorial United Methodist Church family for their
willingness to become a
Community Partnership Church;
Pastors who are seeking to revitalize their churches and community.

FOREWORD

For a good part of the last 15 to 20 years, urban communities all across the country have experienced a racially, socially, economically and culturally charged phenomenon called gentrification. It is the reality where a group of people buy into a poor, declining neighborhood at a lower price and build up their blighted homes. The market forces take over and make it virtually impossible for another group of people, many of whom have lived in that community all their lives, to stay there let alone buy back into the neighborhood. Displacement occurs, preferences shift, coffee shops and dog parks appear and poof! The transformation is on.

From Washington, DC to Atlanta, to Chicago, to Houston, to Los Angeles, to Oakland, gentrification is the reality of the day. And typically, it is wealthy white adults or young white millennia's with great jobs or supportive parents who are leading the charge into these shifting communities. And it is African Americans of all ages, or Latinos of all ages who are being displaced or who are trying to make a quick buck as they see the trend happening and seek to cash in. What emerges from all of this movement is a great deal of tension between races, community groups, politicians, business owners and the like who struggle to keep communities together. There are many Blacks and Latinos who fight to or are financially able to "hold on" or "buy in," and many Whites and other ethnicities who just want a "nice convenient place to live."

Even the church finds itself in the middle of the struggle. For as neighborhoods shift from people of color to predominately white, churches that have been anchors in these neighborhoods for years, find gentrification directly impacting them. The market forces led by wealthy, white suburban congregations to "plant" new faith communities in these changing urban neighborhoods is very strong and many ethnic churches find themselves moving to communities in the suburbs where their parishioners have fled, or staying in the city just trying to make it.

Some of this activity of gentrification is flat out sinful; some is simply the changing of the times. But few people by and large and few churches rarely try to create a bridge between people in the changing communities to see if strong community partnerships can be created and deep binding relationships established between those moving in and those seeking to stay.

All of which makes the work of the Rev. Helen Fleming so important and so rich. As a pastor of a predominantly Black church in a rapidly gentrifying neighborhood in Washington, DC, she and her congregants have decided not to run, but instead to partner. They are working to see where a win-win, can in fact, come to pass. In this handbook entitled, Developing Community Partnership, Helen shares her story and her expertise on how people and churches engulfed in this very tense phenomenon called gentrification can find hope, and partnership in the midst of market forces that divide people for a lifetime. As her superintendent, colleague and friend, I'm proud to see Helen chase this work. It is revolutionary, particularly in times, where racial and economic tensions continue to escalate. More leaders finding ourselves in these changing realties need to chase this work just the same.

Dr. Joseph W. Daniels, Jr.
Greater Washington District Superintendent
Baltimore Washington Conference
The United Methodist Church
Lead Pastor
Emory United Methodist Church
Washington, DC

ACKNOWLEDGEMENTS

I thank Dr. Joseph Daniels for his support in allowing me to be creative in restoring Douglas Memorial United Methodist Church that is now operating under Douglas Worship Center Ecumenical Parish.

I thank Rev. Kevin Lum, the pastor of Table Church and Director of Inspire DC, who has assisted me in creating and developing one church with two missions.

I thank Dr. Rodney Smothers, a Leadership Coach who has assisted me to tear down personal barriers in developing new systems for community partnership.

I thank Athokia Garnett, the CEO of Brandbuilders whose suggestions helped me to highlight key elements of presentation that has made this book informative.

I thank David Wilson for photographing my picture.

I thank Jacqueline Brown, a member of Douglas Memorial United Methodist Church who has helped in the formatting of this book.

I thank Cora Marshall and Christine Kumar who took their time, skills and their love to edit this book.

INTRODUCTION

<u>Rebuilding the Walls in the Urban Cities</u>

Nehemiah 2:18 Let us rise up and build. Then they set their hands to this good work.

In 2005, I was assigned to Douglas Memorial UMC in Washington, DC. The church had experienced a split in the congregation and only 19 members remained. The building was dilapidated and was located on the corner of a business district going through commercial revitalization.

This broken church was also surrounded by a community going through a gentrification process that was changing the area from an African American community to a multi-cultural and multi-racial young professional neighborhood.

Gentrification had caused a downward spiral effect on many of the African American churches. In the community by day, there are homeless, the unemployed and people who are in a survival mode on the streets. By night, the young professionals are socializing in this new strip of pubs, clubs and restaurants.

How does the black church survive during this type of transition? As a prototype in Washington, DC that has been affected by gentrification, our first step was to sell the one piece of property that was owned by the church. This move of faith began the restoration process of revitalizing this blighted building. We realized that the renovation of this building had brought hope and healing to our congregation.

In the urban cities of America, there is a need to build a bridge to connect the existing residents to the emerging new multi-cultural, multi-racial community together. This transition is changing the environment economically and racially. Therefore, this bridge must be built on a new foundation by identifying new methods where all ethnicities can join together and build a new city. This is a vital part of a restoration process in a changing environment.

Developing joint ministries are also vital to restoring the life of the church during this season of transformation. It is critical that a new mind-set takes place in order to effectively communicate to the various cultures, in order to build a bridge that will close the gap between race, age, and culture.

Through Community Partnership/shared ministries, we understand the past environment; however, we are concentrating now on joining forces with the current environment in an effort to restore racial relationships.

We are beginning to meet the needs of all people, present and future generations of all races through Community Partnership. The need for mutual respect is being established with one another in order to fulfill God's purpose for this generation. This unified effort can only manifest when all parties are participating in open communication. That's why we have established the concept of Community Partnership.

Through Community Partnership, we are building multiple ministries in the church; racial reconciliation and healing to our people. Our church, like many other urban churches, has gone through personality differences, many forms of racism and cultural adjustments. We are surpassing those problematic areas through communicating with honesty, love and dedication to the purpose. We must go forward and not look back. We must allow God to be the center of all negotiations for change so that we can develop a unified effort and be on one accord. Building the bridge to Community Partnerships is the way to imitate the God we serve, the God of all people. God makes no mistakes.

This handbook is based on statistics gathered from 19 years of experience as a lead pastor and Executive Director of the Community Partnership, a guide/coach to 18 churches, five years of residency in Washington, DC and the U.S. Census Bureau.

CHAPTER ONE

PURPOSE OF COMMUNITY PARTNERSHIP

The purpose of community partnership or shared ministries has been designed to enhance the urban churches in its separatism that is evolving within our neighborhoods due to gentrification. This concept is also focused on bringing healing to racism and to glorify God's people as we yield all personal agendas and become the Body of Christ.

The sharing of this prototype or example of a typical inner city black church syndrome will reveal the strength and effectiveness of a church engaged in Community Partnership/shared ministries.

This transition is taking place in the inner city of Washington, DC, that was once a predominantly African American urban community and is now an international city of all ethnicities.

Gentrification is rapidly taking over the city of Washington, DC and many other urban cities. The Merriam Webster dictionary defines gentrification as the process of renewing and rebuilding accompanying the influx of middle class influent people into a deteriorating area that often displace poor residents. This experience can be overwhelming to the current residents and neighborhood churches.

Our Black churches have to focus on developing outreach ministries that are inclusive. We have to embrace our new neighbors with the love of God and not to continue to be a separate church unwilling to share.

In some instances, the new residents are not willing to be neighborly or they are resisting neighborly gestures. We are witnessing racial disparity and racial walls existing in many of our communities in our urban cities. It has been said that Sunday morning service is the most racist hour in our country.

As an example, there has been an issue happening within the community, such as, a banner that was hanging outside of the black church inviting Women Veterans to come in for services and support. The new neighbors requested that the banner be removed, because it was not appealing to its new residents and the overall appearance of the neighborhood. Another situation was when there were white youth from all over the country who visited a church in transition to go out and do mission work in shelters, Salvation Army and other places in need of volunteers. However, the new community residents protested against the youth being housed in the area. The youth had to relocate to another community, because it was said that they made too much noise in their neighborhood.

Very often we assume that other races do not want to fellowship in a black or white church; however, the black church put up walls of rejection or they become extremely territorial. African Americans often feel that this is their heritage, and their safe haven. However, God's plan is to heal the racial disparity and restore His churches white and black to oneness. Jesus died for all of us regardless of our race, color or creed. We are the Body of Christ; we are one. It is time for us to let go of the past and walk in unconditional love.

CHAPTER TWO

THE DEMOGRAPHICS

Washington, DC is no longer a "Chocolate City." The economy and demographics are changing daily. According to the Census Bureau, the Black population is decreasing in the residential and business districts by one percent yearly. There is a 38 percent increase of young White professionals moving into the community. The Census Bureau is also projecting a one percent increase of Caucasian residency yearly as well.

Gentrification is drastically changing even in the physical appearance of the city as we turn into an international city. There are new housing developments on every corner to include, high rise apartment buildings and restoration of old row houses. For instance, new businesses are saturating the old business district that was once known as the H Street Corridor with local neighborhood corner stores.

As a point of reference, Washington, DC, had a population of 60 percent African Americans before 2010 and now the population has decreased to 50 percent. The Census Bureau is expecting a continued decrease. In the black community, there is also a ten percent decline of African American home ownership in Washington, DC, while there is 30 percent increase of home ownership among other races.

In areas where transition is high, many of the people of African American decent are now homeless, elderly or living in low-income housing developments. This issue has become a catastrophe.

However, several African American churches were wise to have purchased several properties years ago. I just witnessed a church that negotiated with developers to sell those properties at a great profit.

Many of the Mom and Pop businesses were being encouraged to sell by real estate agencies so that developers could build high rise apartment buildings. This revitalization plan forces the former property business owners to leave due to increases in property taxes and the total cost of living is increasing.

The new residential owners are remodeling the original properties and this has raised the property value in that neighborhood. For example, on the block that Douglas Memorial UMC is located, 90% of the homes in the community are now renovated and owned by Caucasians and other nationalities. The business district is being revived with pubs, restaurants, unique shops, banks, markets and liquor stores by new developers.

One of the largest and prosperous areas of transformation is the H Street corridor in northeast Washington, DC where row houses are purchased at approximately $400,000 and re-sold for $800,000 to $1.5 million. In the Trinidad area, developers have purchased houses unseen for $400,000. Real estate is booming and apartments are rapidly being built wherever there is available property for sale. A studio apartment with 600 sq. ft. is leasing for $1,200 per month, a one bedroom/den with 800 sq. ft. is leasing for $2,400 per month and a two bedroom/two baths with 900 to 1,200 sq. ft., is leasing for $3,000 to 3,700 per month.

Many persons, single head of the household, families, low-income or the elderly can no longer afford to live in the city at these upscale rates. It is more inviting for the African American families who are living on minimum wage or fixed income to sell their properties and move to areas where they can obtain more affordable housing in the suburbs.

Due to this residential change in the community, there is another major issue that needs to be addressed. Parking is in a critical state in this city during the revitalization process. It is almost impossible to find parking for the church family. These parking issues are plaguing the inner city residents of all ethnicities. Many of the new residents are a two car family; therefore, commuters wanting to attend the Black churches are discouraged to come into the city. A lack of parking spaces on Sunday morning or during the week for the commuters to attend church services is a dilemma. The new parking regulations that are being enforced have become a financial deficit specifically to the average church member. Some of my members are receiving more than one ticket per month.

Several of the neighborhoods that were previously minority-based, now have two to four hour parking meters or a residential zone permit. The church that is part of the community is not eligible to receive a parking permit sticker; not even for the pastors. Therefore, each community must begin to seek a solution for this problem.

In conversing with other leaders in several major cities, such as, Philadelphia, Chicago and Baltimore, I found that churches are witnessing a similar loss of African American population and church membership. Those residents who have stayed in the city are lifetime members of other Black churches. Therefore, with the gentrification process moving into the black neighborhoods, the churches have to initiate a plan of action to embrace and recruit all of God's children. There have been very few minority people left to evangelize because what was once an African American community in this vicinity no longer exists.

This reminds us of the Nehemiah movement to restore a city. One of the key elements of the Nehemiah movement is that he pursued God's perfect order before the vision could take place. He shared the vision with the King and requested a leave of absence from his present position. The vision was to rebuild the city wall in Jerusalem. His King gave him permission and support to go forth.

Nehemiah evaluated the situation in order to have a strong plan of action. Then he called the city leaders together and informed them of his plan to rebuild the wall. They recruited volunteers and began to rebuild. They were aware that there were those against them, however, they were prepared for an attack or warfare to bring them down from the wall before it was complete. There was trickery in an attempt to bring Nehemiah down from the wall as well. However, they were equipped and consistent in their assignment and they succeeded in their mission. The walls were rebuilt.

The Challenges in Rebuilding

Metaphorically, we are experiencing challenges in many of our churches. The struggles might appear to be different, but many of our churches can resonate with these unique systemic problems.

Most church properties are in need of repairs and with the loss of membership there are no funds to maintain the property. God's church must be inviting to all generations and races. Our churches should be the center of hope for all people. We need to embrace each other in outreach mission ventures and develop ways to come together to build a new vibrant community. Being of one mind set is critical to the stability of any rapidly changing neighborhood.

The church needs to be an instrument to educate their neighbors on understanding the richness of embracing the diversity within our differences. This is the most exciting part of building partnerships in urban cities.

Also, this is an opportunity to build God's image and to exemplify His characteristics to a new generation. We must stay on the wall until this mission of healing racism and closing the gap between generations is fulfilled.

CHAPTER THREE

THE ROLE OF PRAYER

*James 5:16 The effective fervent prayer
of the righteous availeth much.*

Prayer has to be the center of hope for the transformation of any community development plan that incorporates the church. This plan should never be developed without seeking God for directions. *Mathew 6:33 "Seek ye first the Kingdom of God and His righteousness and all these things shall be added unto you."*

God tells us in Prov. 29:18, "Without a vision my people perish." Then He tells us in Hab. 2:2 "Write the vision and make it plain on a tablet." We should encourage the people to find their place within the vision in order for the vision to be successful.

As we gather data required in the natural to make a quality decision, we also must continue to seek God's face in order to proceed with the vision.

Prayer Structure:

1. Recruit intercessors to take this project to the throne of God to better understand the vision.

2. Share the vision with the team in order for them to find their role within the vision.

3. Seek God for the right structure for your church and for your existing community.

4. Seek God for resources, finances and community partners.

5. Ask God to bring those persons who are compatible and determined to bring the vision to fruition.

6. Pray for the congregations to embrace the concept of Community Partnership.

7. Recognize that there will be fears of losing their religion, traditions and rituals within the congregations as we build partnerships in ministry.

8. Pray for healing for those afraid of a church takeover by other races.

9. Pray that people will reveal their feelings about racism.

10. Pray and fast for racial healing

In the Book of Acts 10:34 says, "God is no respecter of persons," however, insecurity shows its ugly face which stems very often from a spirit of rejection and fear. At the same time, a spirit of superiority can be a stumbling block for those who feel that their answer is the only way for everything. We need to pray for a spirit of humility that will change the hearts of people toward equality with an open mind to accept others as they are.

As the team continues to surrender to God's plan for unity among His people, healing will take place slowly and the old symptoms of hatred and discord will pass away. *(2 Cor. 5:7) "For we walk by faith, not by sight."*

Prayer must be consistent and the center of every meeting in developing the different stages or to maintain the longevity of this life changing experience. This concept depends on the prayer life of all people, because trusting in God is the answer.

Prayer will also continue to build team ethics, character, respect and love for all people. All ministries, groups or persons involved in community Partnership must prayerfully submit to keeping the covenant between all parties. Being involved in this collaborative venture, there needs to be prayer and a spirit of compromise. The agreement will make this a successful model for others to imitate if we are committed to building a racially balanced community.

We need to continue to seek God to see if there are any hidden prejudices still existing within ourselves. *(Ps. 139:23-24) "Search me O Lord and know my heart, try me and know my thoughts. And see if there is any wicked way in me and lead me in the way everlasting."* Racism and hatred has plagued this country too long. Jesus died for all people of all colors.

We must be aware that the adversaries' purpose is to keep God's people separated. Even today, racism is still very much alive. It is up to the Believer to pray and break the generational curse of hatred and division, because we are more than conquerors in Christ Jesus. Prayer changes things.

Remember, our purpose is to make Disciples for Christ. God sees no color.

CHAPTER FOUR

VOICE OF REASONING

How do we keep our churches alive and vibrant when we are no longer a black or white community? The African American traditional churches are dying in the urban cities. Consequently, we must be focused on the bigger picture; we must recognize that we are a part of the whole body of Christ, whether Caucasian, African American, Asian, Hispanic, Indian or other ethnic groups.

In the midst of the changes occurring in our cities, we must first lay a strong foundation by acknowledging God's word that directs us to walk in unconditional love. This is the main ingredients to guide us through the reconstruction and reorganizational process. We are God's representatives on this earth, there should be no color barriers, because God loves all people. This could be God's way of saying, wake up churches and join forces in order to conquer the adversarial spirit of division among our races.

I repeat, that the most racist hour in the church is Sunday morning service. There should not be a Black or White church, but a community church that is there to serve everyone.

After visiting several predominantly Caucasian new church plants in the area, I discovered that this new generation, whether White or Black is not seeking for religion, tradition or rituals, they are seeking a relationship with Jesus Christ.

As we resonate upon these high profile issues confronting each of us, we must not take the easy road to repairing the breach, but recognize that racism puts a crack in the wall that needs repair. When the gifts and talents of each race are acknowledged and embraced by all people, then respect for each other will manifest amongst us.

God has a plan and we must seek Him in each community to determine how to integrate our churches to become more inclusive and tear down the walls of modern segregation. The pastors must keep the congregations involved in the decision making process during this type of transition.

The Kingdom of God according to the Word of God is not racially divided with prejudice and hidden hatred. Truly, there is a need for us to put into practice what we preach. We have to meet each other in the middle of the road knowing that God loves us just the way we are. Let us look at all people through His eyes.

In this generation, we have to rise above our past and rebuild the bridges of not mine or yours, but ours. Whatever the cause might have been that has created this monster; we all have suffered severely the pain of racism over the years in different ways. It is time to let go of the pain of racial discord and realize that God wants us to bring the Kingdom of God on earth as it is in Heaven.

Community Partnership is a method to rebuild the bridge of hope in a racially mixed community. Somehow, we must recognize that forgiveness is the key element needed to have a life changing experience and join forces to rebuild the walls that will heal our nation. With God as our forerunner, we cannot take this dividing spirit of racism into the new millennium. To remove the hidden anger or to circumvent racial amenity, we must be in the midst of re-establishing a congenial relationship regardless of the color of our skin. If we say that we love God, we must accept the fact that this is the will of God.

In the book of Acts chapter 2 when 120 people were on one accord in the upper room, they received the Holy Spirit and they began to speak in other tongues as the Holy Spirit gave them utterance. There were devout Jews from different nations who were in amazement when they heard their language being spoken by the Galileans. God used

Peter to share the upper room experience with them and 3,000 people from all nations accepted Jesus Christ as Lord. They came together as one with all of their differences. As a result of Peter's actions; the first church was born. A multi-racial, multi-cultural church began to worship together. This example of inclusiveness is the will of God for today's generation. The body of Christ is of all races.

"ONE PEOPLE — ONE CHURCH" SELF EVALUATION

When was the last time that you encountered racism?

_____

_____

_____

_____

Are you non-biased or opinionated in your views of other races?

_____

_____

_____

_____

As a minority in this country, do you feel rejected by other races? If so, how are you being healed of your insecurity? In 1 John 4:4, the Bible says, "Greater is He that is within you, then he that is in the world."

_____

_____

_____

_____

When have you thought or said a racist or prejudiced statement?

_____

_____

_____

_____

As a majority in this country, is there a feeling of superiority toward other races because of your heritage? If so, how are you seeking to change knowing that "God is no respecter of persons" (Acts 10-3)?

_____

_____

_____

_____

As a pastor, is there a need to check for racism within the congregation and plan to address the situation?

_____

_____

_____

_____

How do we begin to compromise our differences?

_____

_____

_____

_____

Am I a racist? If so, have I repented to God for my ways and actions?

_____

_____

_____

_____

Are you able to see God's gifts in other ethnicities? Do you judge others based on your expertise or cultural background or beliefs?

_____

_____

_____

_____

Racism is not based on the color of your skin; it is a heart problem in all races. All of us have suffered with pride, rejection, hurt and fear from our past lives. If we don't walk in forgiveness and unconditional love for one another with humility, we cannot build God's Kingdom on earth as it is in Heaven. Again, I say, forgiveness is the healer of racism.

CHAPTER FIVE

HOW TO REBUILD THE WALLS

Neighborhood surveys and social media research are important in understanding the hearts of the people in the business and residential districts.

This information will also help to make decisions on the type of services needed to captivate the residents to come to a worship center. Research will determine whether there should be a traditional and/or a contemporary church service. Neighborhood Bible studies or other educational studies can meet the needs of every gender, age and culture within the community or church.

As an example for services rendered to the community, there should be consideration on whether there is a need for a creative child care center that will be conducive for all residents. Whoever the owners of the child care center, there should be a plan in effect to be inclusive. Also, scholarship funds should be made available for the less fortunate residents.

Advertising through social media is the professional promotional skills needed to initiate communication to the non-church residents as well as members of the existing fellowship. This form of motivational technology can only enhance the interest of those living in the local vicinity.

In order to build a covenant for shared ministries, we must be willing to compromise and stop each group from thinking it must be done a specific way; instead, combine ideas in order to build a joint venture.

There has to be an awareness of each community's own uniqueness and each church needs to be handled with sensitivity and love. We need to address the congregation and leaders with an open mind concept based on their surroundings, traditions and mind-set. Understanding and accepting the differences in cultural behavior can lead to a successful venture.

To be more specific, reasoning with each congregation and listening to their beliefs are part of conquering the existing miss trust that exists in the Black community. The fear of losing control of their historical Black church and a suspicion of a hidden plan for a church takeover by non-Blacks are very much a reality. This behavior happened in my church. My congregation became uncomfortable when their church had an increase of Caucasians in their building on a consistent basis. Comments were made, such as, "They want to take over our building. We don't have any space for our own activities." This was not true; they were not ready to share with another culture because of their own personal history. Therefore, we held racial reconciliation sessions to bring forth honest dialogue and obtaining a better understanding of purpose for each race.

A setting to interact with all parties involved is a vital congregational development process in order to build a community partnership. One of the first steps in building the bridge of unity is placing God's principles in the center of all transactions. This course of action will help to eradicate the emotional subversion and recognize that churches have been a territorial place of refuge. Another key element for all parties to consider while organizing this project is not to dominate one another but to share their gifts with each other. Open discussions and prayer becomes a movement to build mutual respect for the overall church and community development.

Just like Nehemiah, the challenges will be there, but the team cannot come down off the wall or there will be greater problematic issues that will take longer to heal. This is God's plan for His people; move your personal feelings out of the way and glorify God.

CHAPTER SIX

ACCUMULATIVE DATA

An evaluation of the community economic status and demographics will help focus on the homeless, addicted, professional/nonprofessional residents, levels of employment or the unemployed, single head of household, singles, families and youth at the age of reproduction. This methodology will tighten up the plan of action for success by reaching every level of people that is not based on status or the color of one's skin.

EVALUATION PROCESS

Be specific in research and evaluate the accumulated materials in order to design a plan for the Community Partnership project.

Steps of Action:

1. Rally the church members, key community leaders and multi-racial/multi-cultural residents for open dialogue sessions. It is important to have a team of racially balanced participants.

_____

_____

_____

_____

2. Identify what projects are feasible for your church and develop the shared ministries projects accordingly.

_____

_____

_____

_____

3. Develop a strategic team that is dedicated to dealing with the daily issues that are imperative to the longevity of building a solid relationship within shared ministries. Who are the team members in your community?

_____

_____

_____

_____

4. In what ways can you build a bridge for all people to come into agreement on the decision making process of a transitioning neighborhood? What facts must be considered, compromised and agreed upon?

_____

_____

_____

_____

5. If there are two churches with one mission holding two separate services; traditional or contemporary, how would you hold joint services throughout the year to encourage unity among all people?

_____

_____

_____

_____

6. You should check your inner person to see if there's a hidden agenda. If so, what are they?

_____

_____

_____

_____

7. If the church serves as a community center with day care, mission house, special projects, such as, veterans programs, entrepreneurial support services and feeding the homeless. How can Community Partnership be at the center of this collaborative effort?

_____

_____

_____

_____

8. Through social media and other forms of advertisement, publicize your projects for support from the community. How will you promote your project?

_____

_____

_____

_____

9. Be alert for problems in the areas of sharing the sound equipment, double booking of events and sharing of supplies. Develop guidelines with input from each partner in order to eliminate distress or confusion so that the challenges can be solved at the beginning stage.

_____

_____

_____

_____

CHAPTER SEVEN

EXAMPLES OF SHARED MINISTRIES

1. **<u>Mission Group</u>**: The Center for Student Mission brings young students into the urban cities like Washington, DC to serve in shelters and other agencies in need of volunteer services.

2. **<u>Child Care Center</u>**: Toddler's on the Hill has become a part of our partnership. They now have raised funds for scholarship for the underprivileged children in the neighborhood.

3. **<u>Free Summer Camp</u>**: The Garvey Institute is a non-profit organization that mentors and support children whose parents are unable to afford child care for the summer.

4. **<u>Arts Program</u>**: The National Conservatory of Music and Arts are offering classes in music, dance and the arts to the surrounding community. They also provide scholarships to the underprivileged.

5. **<u>The Church Ministries</u>**: A thrift store, the Douglas grocery store operated by shared ministries, lunch for the homeless, a Women's Veteran Resource Center, Leadership Development seminars and professional business and social etiquette sessions for youth, veterans and others seeking careers.

CHAPTER EIGHT

SOCIAL EVENTS AND ACTIVITIES

Christian social activities will help to build relationships within the church and neighborhood. Events for all ages will keep the church visible and more inviting to the community.

Some examples are:

- Christian Jazz Concerts
- Seminars and Workshops
- Music Concerts
- Christian Fashion Shows
- Social and Business Etiquette Sessions
- Rites of Passage for young boys
- Praise Dance and Music Classes
- Arts and Crafts Classes
- Free Summer Camps
- Spiritual Education Conferences
- Seminars/Workshops on various related topics
- Neighborhood Bible studies
- Educational Retreats
- Youth and Children Events
- Veterans job fairs
- Crab feasts
- Bazaars

Collaborative ventures with City, State and Federal agencies will also make the church more conducive and inclusive to the general public. We must always remember that the main purpose of the church is to make disciples for Christ for the transformation of the world.

2 Chron.7:14 If my people who are call by my name will humble themselves and pray, and seek my face and turn from their wicked ways, and then will I hear from heaven, and will forgive their sin and will heal their land.

CHAPTER NINE

PROPERTY EVALUATION

Evaluate the condition of the property.

1. How many people can the building accommodate?

_____

_____

_____

_____

2. What are the assets and liabilities of the building?

_____

_____

_____

_____

3. What are the physical conditions of the building?

_____

_____

_____

_____

4. Is the appearance of the building welcoming?

_____

_____

_____

_____

5. How many ministries can be accommodated in order to book multiple uses out of the same space?

_____

_____

_____

_____

6. Does your building meet the fire codes and the health department regulations in order to fulfill the unified purpose?

_____

_____

_____

_____

7. Is the property handicap accessible?

_____

_____

_____

_____

8. What type of repairs are needed to restore the interior or exterior of the building?

_____

_____

_____

_____

9. Are there showers in the building?

_____

_____

_____

_____

10. Are there enough classrooms, storage or office space?

_____

_____

_____

_____

11. How many exits are located in the building?

_____

_____

_____

_____

12. Is there proper exterior and interior lighting and signs?

_____

_____

_____

_____

13. Do you have an Occupancy Certification?

_____

_____

_____

_____

14. Is there a need for a lift or elevator in your building?

_____

_____

_____

_____

CHAPTER TEN

STRUCTURING A COMMUNITY PARTNERSHIP

The team who has worked to put this project into action has to develop a partnership structure that will keep the daily routine functioning properly. Strong spiritual leadership skills are imperative, instead of positional leadership skills. The sensitivity of nurturing the emotions of others during these transitions is a necessary gift of compassion needed to maintain the joy of the Lord that is their strength.

A Word of Wisdom: If you don't nurture a negative situation and don't allow others to rehearse it, then God will reverse it.

If you have identified the different entities interested in moving into the church facility, there must be a process to monitor the shared ministry and community partnership that will be beneficial to all parties.

QUESTIONS FOR A SUCCESSFUL MERGER

QUESTION: How do you maintain a collaborative effort in the development of a professional and spiritual ministry?

RECOMMENDATION: Strong spiritual leadership with communication skills that has experience in negotiating.

_____

_____

_____

_____

QUESTION: What umbrella are you going to operate under?

RECOMMENDATION: A non-denominational cooperative parish or denomination Worship Center

_____

_____

_____

_____

QUESTION: Will it be an ecumenical setting?

RECOMMENDATION: The doctrines should be acceptable to each party.

_____

_____

_____

_____

QUESTION: How are you going to delegate the space?

RECOMMENDATION: Designate the space based on the effectiveness of service rendered.

QUESTION: How are you going to control schedule events?

RECOMMENDATION: Design a Google master calendar for every entities input.

QUESTION: If it is a new ministry, will you allow them to set up their financial donation on a scale until their ministry is at a stable place with in a time limit?

RECOMMENDATION: Using God's entrepreneurial skills, realize that the benefits might not be at the beginning of each venture, however sowing good seeds will bring back a greater harvest.

QUESTION: Will there be a board or council developed so that all will have a voice when making decisions on transitions that will occur in the church or community?

RECOMMENDATION: Identify an Executive Director to coordinate the functions of the joint efforts. All suggestions will be discussed and recommendations will be voted upon. When there is an unsolved situation, the lead pastor of the building will make the final decision for the betterment of the existing congregation.

_____

_____

_____

_____

QUESTION: Will there be racial reconciliation sessions held regularly until the healing process of deep routed pain of prejudices has been conquered?

RECOMMENDATION: The building of a multi-racial and multi-culture community can only grow if there is honest dialogue, forgiveness, understanding the diversity and accepting the differences as a blessing and not a curse.

_____

_____

_____

_____

QUESTION: What will be the methods for problem solving during this transition in order to enhance a long term healthy relationship?

RECOMMENDATION: Complications occur and must be solved, accusatory statements are not acceptable during these sessions. All parties are asked to recommend a solution for every situation or problematic issues that occur during this partnership.

—————————————————————

—————————————————————

—————————————————————

—————————————————————

QUESTION: What form of evaluation will be designed to learn the positive effects from this experience and to enhance the success of shared ministries?

RECOMMENDATION: Shared ministries within Community Partnerships are a vital part of reconciling a multi-racial community. If the various entities truly work together with authenticity and then stay on one accord to build a stronger community, this project will be a success. This type of transformation will produce new life for its people.

—————————————————————

—————————————————————

—————————————————————

—————————————————————

QUESTION: How do we combine the new millenium generation with the somewhat traditional generation?

RECOMMENDATION: Recognizing that the existing generation throughout the Bible embraced the emerging generations in order to walk in victory.

—————————————————————

—————————————————————

—————————————————————

—————————————————————

CHAPTER ELEVEN

SPIRITUAL LEADERSHIP

SPECIFICATIONS FOR THE EXECUTIVE DIRECTOR

The person serving as an Executive Director to the Community Partnership should be one who can coordinate, organize, and communicate the vision. They should be spiritually grounded in the Word of God and walking in his/her call to ministry. This person's core values must not be compromised. Strong negotiation skills are vital to the process in partnering. A warm, yet, aggressive personality is crucial to connecting all of the entities and maintaining the relationships.

PROBLEM SOLVING SKILLS

Community Partnership has many problematic areas to be resolved. Flexibility in decision making is vital to connecting the barriers that sometimes lay between race, culture and age differences. Keeping open dialogue eliminates division and a negative conclusion without allowing each party to have words of expression, is a necessity. An accusatory complaint without a solution does not bring unity among partners. Always advocate for solutions when solving partnership problems.

<u>ADMINISTRATIVE PREVENTIVE MEASURES</u>

- Partnership meetings should be scheduled regularly.

- Rules should be set by all parties in order to keep disagreements and confusion at a minimum.

- The most important process to be enforced is not to allow an accusatory spirit to control a meeting.

- Shut down negative responses within the shared ministries that could be detrimental to the mutual relationships between the partners.

- Seek God for wisdom in finding solutions to the problems especially personality clashes.

- Challenges are usually around time, space, shared music instruments, sound systems and the opinions of the congregants concerning the dramatic invasion of the unfamiliar.

- The congregation must be kept informed of what is taking place in the building to eliminate damaging conversations that are thoughts and not truth.

- All recommended changes should be reported to all entities immediately and documented.

- Make sure that leaders from all entities have an opportunity to meet and greet, because this will help with the feeling of not belonging or being isolated.

- Team building is important to the body of Christ during this joint effort.

- The Google calendar must be kept up-to-date by all parties in shared ministries.

- Professionalism in organizing or planning of events among all groups is the answer to a successful merger.

- The leader should hold consistent racial reconciliation sessions to keep the tension of cultural differences or intentional negative behavior under control.

- Each person's culture sends different responses and perspectives that are not always understandable. Show them grace and compassion.

CHAPTER TWELVE

BENEFITS OF COMMUNITY PARTNERSHIP

When a church extends itself beyond its walls to support a transitional community, it brings opportunities to obtain funds to create other needed programs for the betterment of the surrounding areas.

When you are engulfed in outreach ministries, such as, services for veterans, day camp, feeding the homeless and a grocery store for the poor; then funds are available for the church to take ministries to higher levels.

Community recognitions, such as the White House acknowledgements, media coverage and federal or city government support will enlarge your territory. Funders can see that you are improving the neighborhood by showing compassion and love in rebuilding the community. They must be able to trust you which will add clout to your organizations track record. Local business will offer support to a variety of programs.

These projects open opportunities to shared pulpits with other denominations and races that will broaden your experiences. Joint activities on Holy holidays become mutual ministries with a mixed congregation; for instance, we have two churches with one mission that is housed in this Community Partnership. We held a Seven Last Words service with two White churches and one Black church. It was highly successful as we shared Words of Expression together.

This family atmosphere shows there are no differences when we are in worship; we become God's people praising Him together. This gathering opened the door for God to do miraculous things.

Through the recognitions received by serving the community, brought forth in-kind benefits that can excel the partnership efforts beyond expectations.

Examples of Support:

- White House for Veteran and Partnership Affairs.
- Home Depot Foundation
- Mayor's Office of Veteran Affairs
- H Street Merchant Association
- George Washington University Veterans Program
- Department of Labor
- Court Services and Offenders Supervision Agency
- Federal Women's Veterans Affairs
- Concerned Black Men
- Department of Employment Services, Project Empowerment Program
- Media Coverage
- Veteran's Hospital
- Garvey Institute

These projects open opportunities to share with other denominations and communicate with other races that will broaden the exposure of Community Partnership. Joint activities on Holy holidays become mutual ministries with a mixed congregation becoming one in Christ. These gatherings also opened the door for God to do miraculous things.

CHAPTER THIRTEEN

MUTUAL AGREEMENTS

After spending time in prayer, research and using our business sense, it was decided to never rent God's house, but to trust God for the increase as we seek His guidance on every step of the way during this new venture.

We identified an agreement called a Memorandum of Understanding (MOU).

HOW DO WE DESIGN THE MOU?

The pastor and the congregation will create and sign-off on the MOU and Covenant with each entity. This system should be approved by the pastor, District Superintendent or head of the denominations. The pastor can serve as the lead pastor and the executive director of the daily operations or a person can be delegated as the coordinator of the projects. A person assigned by the pastor will be responsible for the income and the distribution of the financial revenue in order to care for the property and obtain items that are needed to maintain the function of the ministries with excellence.

Many of the inner city churches are in a desperate need for physical restoration and revitalization. One of the assets of Community Partnership is the joint participation in caring for the overall restoration of the building together. When we join forces, each party identifies areas of their strengths that will enhance the restoration process of these blighted buildings that give a sense of shared ministries or partnership.

It is apparent that God is saying to the present church, we can no longer maintain our buildings alone. We are one in Christ, all races and all cultures. He is forcing us to reach out beyond our natural capabilities or capacity and realize it takes all the gifts of God's people working together to rebuild the wall to God's kingdom living.

NOTE: Nehemiah called those whom he trusted, faithful and obedient to authority to rebuild the city.

Previously, the lead pastor has served in more than one capacity. The Executive Director of an ecumenical cooperative parish community partnership and the lead pastor of the local church is the overseer of these model projects. These dual positions can become overwhelming. The responsibility includes; racial reconciliation sessions, determining who will blend with the existing ministries, delegating space, overseeing schedules, building relationships among all entities, responding to complaints, coordinating joint activities and mentoring the various ministries. However, it has been under consideration that we delegate a neutral person to be identified as the Executive Director to oversee and coordinate all of the shared ministries projects.

SAMPLE
MEMORANDUM OF UNDERSTANDING

This Memorandum of Understanding (Generic Agreement) is made by _____church and between _____ having its principle offices at_____and_____ church having principle offices at _____. The parties have entered into this MOU to implement and collaborate with an ecumenical cooperative agreement based upon the principles of your denomination. As such, the parties agree to the following:

In consideration of the mutual covenants and promises contained herein and intending to be legally bound, the parties agree as follows:

1. <u>MUTUAL COVENANT</u>:

This agreement is to operate under the umbrella of _____ _____ and join forces with the _____ in an effort to further serve and enrich the community. The purpose of building an Ecumenical Cooperative Parish is to embrace a multi-racial and multi-cultural generation entering our community and to further God's kingdom.

1. Shared Use of Building
    a. The building will be available to _____ daily from_____ to _____ five days a week and on Saturday from _____to _____.
2. Congregations will share use of building to be facilitated by the joint council and shared calendar.
3. Relationship Development

      a. Purpose is to expose the community and congregants to diversity in ministry.

4. Joint Church Council

      a. Church Council to include a pastor, a finance person, trustee and one other member from each congregation.

5. Ordination

      a. Individuals interested in ministry can choose to pursue ordination with the present congregation.

2. <u>PERIOD OF MOU</u>:

The Memorandum of Understanding shall commence on _____ and continue indefinitely, until termination by either party with a 60-day notice.

3. <u>COMPENSATION AND PAYMENT</u>: (Church Agreement)

The _____ Church agrees to contribute 30% of its revenue to support _____church and its ministries up to fair market rental value. Then additional money will be put into a joint ministry budget to be administered by the council.

4. <u>SACRAMENTS</u>:

Both congregations agree that there are two sacraments ordained of Christ our Lord, those are Baptism and the Lord's Supper. Furthermore, we agree that sacraments are not only budget or tokens of Christian men or women professions, but are signs of grace and God's good will towards all mankind.

Baptism is not only a sign of profession and marks of differences whereby Christians are distinguished from others that are not baptized, but it is also a sign of regeneration or new birth. Baptism is offered to both children and adults. The Lord's Supper is a sign not only of the love Christians ought to have for one another, but also a sacrament of our redemption by Christ's death. The Lord's Supper is open to all who realize they are in need of God's Grace.

5. ORDINATION:

Both congregations agree that ordination is a gift from God to the church. In ordination, the church affirms and continues the apostolic ministry through persons empowered by the Holy Spirit. As such, those who are ordained make a commitment to conscious living of the whole gospel and to the proclamation of the gospel to the end of time that the world may be saved.

Individuals interested in ordinations can pursue ordination through either ecclesial body.

6. TERMINATION:

This Memorandum of Understanding shall not be terminated without the express written agreement of both parties. If_____ terminates the Memorandum of Understanding; the_____ shall pay _____ any building improvements agreed to by the joint council above and beyond anything covered by the 30% with the amount depreciating by 20% per year.

7. MISCELLANEOUS:

This Memorandum of Understanding constitutes the entire agreement between the parties. This Memorandum of Understanding may not be modified or altered except in writing and duly executed by authorized officers of both parties. No other terms and conditions, oral or written, be they consistent, inconsistent, or additional to those contained herein, shall be binding upon parties, unless and until such terms and conditions shall have been specifically in writing by the parties.

The _____ and _____ have agreed to the terms outlined, and has therefore, caused this Memorandum of Understanding to be executed by the authorized officers as set forth below.

_____Date_____   _____Date_____
John Doe   Rev. Dr. Helen Stafford Fleming
Lead Pastor   Executive Director
                                       Lead Pastor
                                       Douglas Memorial UMC
                                       800 Eleventh Street, NE
                                       Washington, DC 20002

SUMMARY

The success of Community Partnership is when all things work together for the good of those who love the Lord who are called according to His purpose. (Rom 8:28) Prayers are answered when we come together on one accord regardless of ethnicity. Let us run the race together and win the victory.

When we share in our diversity, a covenant between all parties will represent our character, ethics and our trust in the Lord. As men and women of God, our commitment to love one another is His greatest commandment that must be adhered to with authenticity. We have an opportunity to exercise our social and business graces as a vital part of building the community and as a result we will bring the Kingdom of God on earth as it is in Heaven.

We, as confessed Believers must repent and reject traits of racial hatred, insecurity or superiority out of our lives before we can bring unity to the Body of Christ. These issues must be explored with open communication and honesty in order to lead the partners through a healing process that is imperative to shared ministries growth with all Believers. God has a master plan to rebuild the hearts of man just like Nehemiah rebuilt the city wall. Unconditional love is the answer to all ills. If we have not love, we have not God. Let us repair the breach of separatism and defeat the enemies so that we can praise God for the victory over division. Give God the glory for the things He has done.

The Greek word for church is Ekklesia, in English Ecclesia which means community. The church is the community.

Finally, the first church was born with 3,000 people from all nations. Let us restore the church of God on earth as it is in Heaven wherever the opportunity arises within our community.

(Isaiah 58:12) Your ancient ruins shall be rebuilt; you shall raise up the foundation of many generations; you shall be called The Repairer of the Breach, the restorer of streets to live in.

"It's always seems impossible until it is done." Nelson Mandela